Santa's Christmas Eve Blues

Published by Long Midnight Publishing, 2024

copyright © 2011 Douglas Lindsay

All rights reserved. No part of this publication may be reproduced or transmitted in any form or by any means without permission of the author.
Douglas Lindsay has asserted his right under the Copyright, Designs and Patents Act 1988 to be identified as the author of this work.
All the characters in this book are fictitious and any resemblance to actual persons, living or dead, is purely coincidental.

ISBN: 979-8346496229

www.douglaslindsay.com

SANTA'S CHRISTMAS EVE BLUES

DOUGLAS LINDSAY

Illustrations by Jess Lindsay

LMP

1

A long time ago at the North Pole, where the weather was always wonderfully snowy and cold, lived Santa Claus. He worked all year round with his team of elves to make toys and games, which he would then distribute amongst all the children of the world in the early hours of Christmas morning. At least, all the children of the world who had been well-behaved.

One of the tasks of Santa's elves was to monitor the day-to-day conduct of children everywhere, checking on whether or not they had been naughty or nice. After twelve months of intelligence gathering, the information would be collated into a series of reports, from which Santa would make a list. He would then check the list on at least two further occasions.

It was a simple life and Santa was content. The population of the world was small, and the expectations of children were low. A doll or a small wooden toy, that was all they'd get in their stocking, and that was all they ever wanted.

But, as we said at the start of the story, that was a long time ago…

The world has changed, the number of people has grown, and it's been years since Santa has been able to run his small operation out of the North Pole. Instead, he's become the powerless figurehead of an enormous global enterprise, The Big Fat Father Christmas Corporation, a division of a huge and faceless international conglomerate, whose headquarters take up every single floor of a ninety-seven storey skyscraper in Manhattan. Along the way, the elves have been replaced by a highly structured administrative chain of command, from the Board of Directors at the top, down through several levels of grey-suited middle and junior management.

It isn't even wonderfully snowy and

cold at the North Pole any longer. Indeed, scientists predict that within ten years, polar bears will be extinct, Greenland will actually have become green, and the ice sheets will have been replaced by coral reefs and barmen named Raoul mixing margaritas.

Worst of all for Santa, there are now over two and a half billion children in the world, and that's an awful lot of children whose behaviour has to be monitored every minute of every day for an entire year. The elves did their best in the past but once the Big Fat Father Christmas Corporation got involved, the operation was put out to tender and the elves were replaced by a giant, multinational security contractor who had invested heavily in AI, drones and spy satellites. Christmas is big business, and can no longer be left in the hands of little people in green outfits.

And what of Santa, now that the nature of Christmas has so evolved? His work has been completely taken over by a string of faceless executives, so that Santa has been reduced to little more than a messenger. Whereas before he worked all year round, making judgement calls on which children deserved presents, and individually selecting gifts for each child, he has become nothing but the delivery boy on

Christmas morning, a task he combines with making the occasional guest appearance at department stores in the weeks leading up to the big day.

And so, over the years, Santa has become more and more fed up and tired, which is how, one year very recently, Christmas itself nearly didn't happen.

2

December 24th that year was a snowy day in New York, which was exactly the kind of day that Santa used to love at the North Pole. Now, however, he was grumpy and old, and the snow just played havoc with his sciatica and made him want to snuggle down with a cup of hot chocolate and watch television.

  Just before nine pm, when he should have been getting ready for his busiest night of the year, Santa was sitting in a comfy chair, his feet on a small coffee table, still dressed in his vest and long johns and staring out at the cold, cold night, as the snow fell over New York. In his hands was a guitar, and as he sat, he strummed a tune full of sorrow and melancholy.

There was a knock at the door, and although Santa did not invite his late evening visitor to enter, the door opened and a young man, wearing this year's spectacles and smelling of *Pantalon Grand Garçon pour Hommes*, confidently walked into the room.

Santa did not look round. His visitor, Executive Vice-President In Charge of Deliveries, Jeff D Sheldrake, stopped and stared. Sheldrake was non-plussed. Sure, he knew how to work a room, and he knew how to sell sand to the Bedouin and ice to the Inuit, but he did not have the necessary skillset that would allow him to deal with a Christmas legend sitting in his underwear playing the guitar.

'Santa?' he said cautiously.

Santa did not reply. Despite the rather grand title, Santa knew that Sheldrake was a very small fish in the exceptionally large pond of The Big Fat Father Christmas Corporation. Others would follow, and Santa did not feel like wasting words, just yet.

'Why, this is extraordinary,' said Sheldrake nervously, but Santa did not respond. Unsure of what was happening, and with the vague feeling that a cataclysmic event was about to take place and that he, Jeff D Sheldrake, would be held responsible, Sheldrake turned and hurried from the room, leaving Santa alone with his guitar and the beautiful white snow falling outside the window.

3

Sheldrake stood waiting anxiously for the elevator, even though he only had to go down to the floor below. Executive Vice-Presidents never took the stairs.

Just below Santa's penthouse apartment, the President of the Board, Henry F Potter, had an office that took up exactly half of the 96th floor. Some said that Potter wanted an office of this size so that he could play golf at lunchtime without needing to drive to his country club in the Hamptons.

In the much smaller office outside, his personal assistant, Miss Kubelik, was not impressed that a junior executive wished to see Potter at this time on Christmas Eve.

'I must impress upon you the urgency of this matter, Miss Kubelik,' said Sheldrake.

'But it's Christmas Eve,' said Miss Kubelik. 'I've just passed around the coffee and the pumpkin pie. Why, the entire floor is like a picture print by Currier and Ives!'

'Miss Kubelik, the very future of Christmas hangs in the balance,' said Sheldrake, his voice beginning to break.

Sheldrake knew how to play an audience.

Miss Kubelik looked like she desperately didn't want to be impressed, but she couldn't help it. Sheldrake had drawn her in, and suddenly she realised that she herself had a part to play in what was clearly a tense and fascinating drama, which might one day be made into a film for television.

'I think he may have a forty-five second window in five minutes,' she said, while still trying to imply disinterest.

This was exactly what Sheldrake needed to hear, though it did not make him any more relaxed.

'Miss Kubelik,' he said, 'those forty-five seconds are going to be the most important forty-five seconds on all the earth since the invention of the gingerbread man.'

Miss Kubelik gasped, and wondered if it was time to set up Netflix and Apple TV on speed dial.

4

Sheldrake paced up and down outside Potter's office, until finally the call came through that the President of the Board was ready to see him. It took him almost another minute to walk from the door to Potter's desk.

'What appears to be the trouble?' said Henry F. Potter cheerily, without looking up from a spreadsheet showing that month's sales figures.

'It's Santa, sir,' said Sheldrake. 'I get the feeling he's not focused on the night ahead. I get the feeling that he might not be going out on his sleigh.'

For a moment Sheldrake wondered if Potter had even heard him, then slowly Potter raised his head and looked at Sheldrake with amused curiosity. He wasn't sure, but these figures were encouraging and he was beginning to think that this December might well turn out to be the best December ever.

'Not focused? But this is his biggest night of the year. If Santa refused to go out on Christmas Eve, why it would be like coffee deciding to taste like tea. It'd be like green eggs and ham, or a coral reef at the North Pole. What seems to be the problem?'

'Well, sir,' said Sheldrake nervously, 'he appears to be singing the blues.'

Henry F Potter raised a dubious eyebrow as the smile disappeared from his face, and then he slowly lifted his enormous frame out of the chair.

A few minutes later Potter stood before Santa Claus, his eyebrow still dubiously raised. Usually at this time on Christmas Eve, Santa would have been all spruced up in his best red and white suit, he would've been standing in front of the mirror checking that his beard was snowy-white, or he would have been ensuring that his reindeer were all preened and ready to fly off into the magical night air from their rooftop location. But Santa was still as Sheldrake had described him, in his underwear, feet on the table, strumming his guitar.

Potter watched him for a few moments, not entirely sure how to proceed. He was glad he had not brought Sheldrake with him, as he did not want a subordinate to see him in such a state of confusion.

'Mr. Claus?' said Potter, eventually stepping forward.

Santa did not turn. He looked out at the snow falling softly over Fifth Avenue, and raised his own dubious eyebrow.

'What appears to be the trouble?'

asked Potter.

Finally Santa turned slowly round and looked at the President of the Board. And then, to Potter's consternation, Santa began to sing:

> *'It's a frosty night.*
> *All snowy and cold.*
> *I'm all out of Prozac,*
> *I feel tired and old.*
> *I ain't puttin' on that outfit,*
> *ain't goin' out on that sleigh,*
> *I hate all those horrible, miserable*
> *children anyway.*
> *They give me the blues,*
> *I've got the blues,*
> *I've got the blues,*
> *I've got the Christmas Eve blues.'*

Henry F Potter stood listening to the song in stupefied silence. He had never heard of such a thing. Santa not wanting to go out on Christmas Eve was like Little Jack Frost refusing to put the bite on your toes.

'Why, this is extraordinary,' said Potter, when Santa had finished singing. 'What on earth did you have for breakfast this morning?'

Henry F Potter might have been alarmed, but Santa did not respond. Instead he continued to strum his guitar, playing a tune full of sorrow and melancholy.

5

Half an hour later Henry F Potter was presiding over a full board meeting of The Big Fat Father Christmas Corporation. Many of the executives had been indifferent about being summoned to work at this late hour on Christmas Eve, but Potter had made sure that Miss Kubelik had impressed upon each of them the extreme urgency of the matter.

'We must find a way to get him to deliver the presents!' cried Potter, slamming his fist onto the table. The smile of affable curiosity from earlier had completely vanished. Once again Potter was the hard-nosed businessman who had once managed to sell rainwater to Scotland.

'Christmas has to happen or shares in this company will collapse overnight. It'll make *Jurassic Park* look like a teddy bear's picnic in a Girl

Scout factory.'

Even though Potter could be a little strange sometimes, and many of the things he said did not actually make any sense, everyone still knew what he meant.

'Why don't we get someone else to do it?' chirped a small round woman from the far end of the table.

There was a sudden, hushed silence, and everyone looked at the small round woman who had dared to speak. Potter did not like it when someone other than him spoke at a board meeting, and a couple of senior executives glanced at him nervously, waiting for the eruption.

'Because,' began Potter slowly, keeping his temper in check, 'Santa has to deliver sixteen billion presents to approximately one billion homes in a very short period of time. Do you know how he does that?'

'No,' said the small round woman, timidly shaking her head.

'Well,' said Potter imperiously, 'neither do I. Nobody does. It's magic, Santa's special magic, and he's the only one who can do it. Of course, we have scientists working on the technology, but they're decades away from a breakthrough. We need answers, people, or this company is going to sink faster than the Titanic in a bowl of custard. We're in permanent danger of losing the Christmas franchise to Amazon, or the

Chinese even, and this will be the catalyst to tip us over the edge. Now, I know there's usually little point in any of you speaking when I'm in the room, but it's time to throw the pigskin into the bushes and set fire to the envelope. We need ideas and we need them in the next ten seconds.'

'Perhaps,' said a strange little man with dimples on his nose, 'we could ask Mrs Claus to have a word with him.'

Potter sat back, his hands clasped on his big, fat belly, a belly engorged on mince pies, spiced eggnog cookies and mulled wine, as he regarded the strange little man with dimples on his nose for some time.

'Mrs Claus,' he said eventually. 'Might work. Might just work.'

The strange little man relaxed and sat back, hoping that his idea might be the one that helped save Christmas.

So it was that soon afterwards, Mrs Claus was flown by helicopter to Manhattan from her retirement home in Saratoga.

6

A short while later, with time running out and Christmas in danger of not taking place at all, Verity Claus walked into the sitting room of her husband's penthouse apartment, to find him in exactly the same position he'd been in for his earlier visitors.

The snow was continuing to fall outside and there was an empty mug of hot chocolate sitting on the table beside Santa, with chocolaty lip marks on the rim from where he had taken his last slurp.

'Why,' said Mrs Claus, 'this is extraordinary.'

Henry F Potter had once remarked that he found talking to Mrs Claus to be like having a conversation with Grace Kelly in a Miss Piggy costume, although it was never absolutely clear from that sentence which one of them was dressed as the Muppet.

Santa gave his wife a glance, then looked back out at the falling snow. He'd long thought his marriage was old enough that he and his wife could understand each other perfectly without ever needing to talk. This was not an opinion that Mrs Claus ever seemed to have shared.

'What about the children?' she asked. 'Don't you realise what you're doing?'

And then, much to Mrs. Claus's consternation, for she had long tired of her husband's penchant for bursting into song, Santa began to sing.

'Don't know 'bout you,
but I could care more.
They ain't gettin' any presents,
That's what they've got in store.
It'll teach them a lesson,
in avarice and greed.
A year without an X-Box
is exactly what they need.
It'll give them the blues,
yeah, they're getting the blues.
They'll get the blues,
They'll get the Christmas Eve blues.'

'Oh, I hate it when he does that,' mumbled Mrs Claus. Then, realising she would get nothing further from her husband, she walked out, intent on collecting the share options she'd been promised in return for trying to change Santa's mind, unaware that within hours the share options wouldn't be worth the candy cane they were written on.

Santa watched the door close, then looked back out at the wintry sky and once more started to strum quietly on his guitar, his heart full of sorrow and melancholy. He thought about the old days, and the good times he had had with the elves. And he wondered where they all were now, because it had been years and years since he had seen any of them.

But thinking of the elves just made him feel even sadder, and so he forced himself to not think of his dear old friends, and instead he decided he had time for one more cup of hot chocolate before bedtime.

7

'Clearly,' said Henry F Potter, at the next emergency meeting of the executive board of The Big Fat Father Christmas Corporation, 'the Mrs Claus Strategy failed to work. It was foolish to have thought it might. Time is short, ladies and gentlemen. We need ideas, or by this time tomorrow we'll all be scraping pigs' trotters from the bottom of the barrel.'

There was almost silence around the room, the only sound the gentle plop of sweat falling to the table from worried brows. The Board were beginning to panic.

'Got it!' said a curiously small man with an exceptionally large moustache, sitting dangerously close to Potter to be expressing such enthusiasm. 'We should ask Mr Gruber to go and see him. That'll do the trick.'

There was an audible gasp around the room, like the sound of pixies bursting from eating too many pfefferkuchen. Mr Gruber was the Ultimate Supreme Dictator For Life of The Big Fat Father Christmas Corporation, and no one, not even Henry F Potter, dared disturb him out of office hours. Not even in an emergency, not even on the 24th December.

Despite his position of executive authority, Mr Gruber had in fact hated the festive season since his brother had died in a mysterious fall from a skyscraper in Los Angeles on Christmas Eve many years previously.

This, however, was an emergency like no other. This, thought Henry F Potter, made the Cuban missile crisis look like a strawberry shortage in a raspberry jam factory.

Potter stared at the curiously small man with the exceptionally large moustache and began to think that perhaps he was right. There really was no other option. He was going to have to get Mr Gruber out of bed.

8

Half an hour later, with his Christmas empire on the verge of collapse, Mr Gruber walked into Santa's sitting room. Santa was sitting in the same position as before, except now there was a new steaming mug of hot chocolate on the table beside him.

Gruber stood with his arms folded and surveyed this unfortunate scene, and was terribly disconcerted. However, just as he was about to speak, Santa caused him even greater distress by breaking into song:

'I'm completely washed up, I'm all out of gas.
This whole Christmas thing, is a pain in the…'

'Enough with the blues, already!' shouted Gruber, interrupting, waving his arms with a Germanic flourish. 'Enough with the blues, enough of this foolishness. You must put on your suit and deliver the presents. Accept your fate, Mr Claus. The world is about capitalism and greed, that is what matters. You have created this monster, so do not pretend that it appals you so. It is you who has fashioned this beast. You must do your duty or, for sure, the entire capitalist structure of the western world will collapse!'

Santa hung his head low and then, much to Gruber's further alarm, he once more burst into song:

'So what you're sayin' is,
I make things worse.
This is all kinds of wrong,
Bein' Santa's a curse.
That don't make me happy,
Don't make me impressed.
The snow's a-fallin' outside
And I ain't gettin' dressed.

'Cause I've got the blues,
yeah I've got the blues.
I've got the blues,
I've got the Christmas Eve blues.'

By the time Santa had finished his lament, Gruber had left the room. Santa hardly even noticed. He didn't care about Mr Gruber. Nor, he had to sadly admit to himself, did he care about Christmas.

9

Shortly afterwards, Mr Gruber presided over the final ever board meeting of The Big Fat Father Christmas Corporation. He stood gloomily at the head of the long table, Henry F Potter at his side, and miserably regarded the room full of frightened executives.

'Ladies and gentlemen,' he began, 'we must not hyperbolise this terrible situation in which we currently find ourselves. Nevertheless, I do not think it too much of an exaggeration to say that Christmas will not be happening this year, that no children anywhere in the entire world will be getting presents – even the very few who have actually been good – that the world's economy will crumble into the dust, and that we will all die, penniless and alone.'

To a man and woman, the board members looked ashen-faced. Someone swallowed, very loudly. A couple of them wondered if it was an appropriate time to start crying.

'Obviously,' continued Mr Gruber, 'when I say that we will all die penniless and alone, I do not include myself. If I were a nation rather than an individual, I would be the third richest country in Europe. Most of you, however, are now destitute and ruined. Your futures are hopeless. Content yourself, however, with this knowledge... You need not worry about me, I will be fine.'

With these heart-warming words, Mr Gruber left the building and was soon being whisked away in his chauffeur-driven Rolls Royce Silver Badger.

Once he was gone, Henry F Potter wondered if he should rally the troops with a stirring Shakespearean soliloquy, however he too had been overwhelmed by this feeling of foreboding.

The Board of Directors looked out of the window at the snow falling softly over Fifth Avenue and sadly packed up their things and prepared to go home. Christmas had been cancelled and life would never, ever be the same again.

10

Up in his penthouse apartment Santa laid down his guitar, stretched massively, took a last sip of hot chocolate, took a final look out at the beautiful falling snow, then went to the bathroom to clean his teeth.

He felt old and tired and jaded. It was true that he had not lost the special magic that allowed him and the reindeer to deliver so many presents to so many children in one night, yet undoubtedly Christmas had lost its magic for him. The days with his elves making wooden toys for appreciative children seemed so long ago.

It had been another age. A golden age, when the world was full of promise. Now the world, and all the children in it, seemed as old and tired and jaded as he himself. Cynicism had swept across the land, bringing with it greed and conceit and narcissism. Santa belonged in a different world. Society had moved on, and it was time for Santa to let go.

He washed his face, changed into his pyjamas and walked into the bedroom. Christmas was over forever and, when he got up in the morning, he could decide what to do in the future instead. He had no idea what that would be, but he did know that it would not involve a red and white suit, a sleigh or any reindeer. And, as he stroked his beard, he wondered if perhaps it was time to shave it off. He couldn't even remember the last occasion he'd seen his chin.

Santa stopped. Sitting on his pillow was a small parcel, wrapped in red, silver and green paper. Santa felt a funny sensation tingling down his spine and, for the first time in a long while, he felt the weight of gloom and sadness lift from his shoulders. Someone had left him a present.

This, in itself, was strange. It had been years since anyone had given Santa a present. People were happy to take from Santa, but no one ever thought to give him anything other than a small glass of milk, or a shot of whisky. Santa liked neither, and no one ever left him a mug of hot chocolate.

He sat down on the edge of the bed and lifted the small package. He studied it, he shook it. It was a book. There was a little gift tag on it, handwritten with immaculate care.

To Santa,
Merry Christmas
From your friends, the Elves

11

Suddenly Santa felt warmer than a cup of hot chocolate. He looked around the room, but the elves were nowhere in sight. He wondered if they'd been here earlier in the day, or whether they were lurking somewhere. They'd always had the knack of surprising him.

  He slowly unwrapped the present. It was a small book with a hard cover. On the front was a picture of two children sitting at the foot of a wonderful and beautifully decorated Christmas tree, unwrapping presents. Their room was adorned in sparkling silvers and golds and there was a large roaring fire. The children were smiling and happy, with their mum and dad watching from the sofa, drinking mulled wine and remembering how wonderful it had been for them when they'd been children. And at the top of the picture was the title of the book: *The Magic of Christmas*.

Santa felt a lump in his throat and looked round, but still there was no one there. He turned back to the book and slowly opened it. Then he sat back and looked on in wonder, for this was no ordinary book. This was a book that delivered what it promised in the title.

As soon as the book was open, the air was filled with the enchanting smells and sounds of Christmas, and his room, which he had steadfastly refused to decorate, suddenly began to fill with glorious sparkle and colour.

Santa could feel the warmth of an open fire; he could smell cinnamon and spices and candles, roast turkey and the pine needles of a real tree; he could smell hot wine and chestnuts roasting, and the wonderful aroma of old Christmas decorations; he had the sweet taste of Christmas cake in his mouth, he could hear the laughter of children and the joyous ring of silver bells. Then all around the room beautiful decorations appeared, in green and red and gold; the fire in the hearth started burning brightly, and in the corner a wonderful tree appeared, the pine needles frosted white and covered in red and silver baubles and tinsel and small angels. It was as if the room had been infused with the distilled essence of Bing Crosby, and Santa suddenly felt warm and happy and really rather wonderful.

And, as he sat with the book open on his lap, the joy of Christmas once more in his heart, he realised what he'd done and how the world would be deprived this night because of him. And suddenly he felt sad, for he had spurned so many of his visitors, he had been so consumed by his own Christmas Eve blues, that it was now too late to venture out into the snowy night. Even with his own incredible special magic, he would never be able to fulfil all his contractual obligations.

And then, to his further astonishment, from behind the tree came four little figures in green. A huge smile came to Santa's face.

'Elves!' he exclaimed, and the elves ran to him and they hugged him.

It had been so long since he'd seen any of them, but they had not changed one bit in all those years.

'Oh my goodness,' said Santa, 'how wonderful! This is all your work?'

'We've been practicing,' said Dudley, the tallest elf. (Although even Dudley wasn't very tall.)

'It's wonderful to see you,' said Santa, 'but what am I to do? I've ruined Christmas!'

'It's not too late,' said Dudley. 'You still have the magic, don't you? Santa's special Christmas magic?'

'Of course,' said Santa.

'Well,' said Dudley, 'come with us to the North Pole. We've been waiting for you all these years, and we have enough presents for you to deliver to all the children.'

Santa's eyes lit up. The North Pole! It was going to be just like the good old days!

12

And so, as the executives of The Big Fat Father Christmas Corporation streamed dejectedly out into the cold night, Santa climbed once more into his red and white suit, checked his beard in the mirror for snowy-whiteness, then went to the shed on the roof of the building where the elves had already hooked up the reindeer to the sleigh.

Santa and the four elves climbed in, the reindeer nodded amongst themselves, relieved that Christmas was indeed going to happen, and then they were on their way to the North Pole to collect the billions of presents that the elves had been accumulating through the years.

'Won't we be too late?' said Santa, as the sleigh took off and sped through the night sky.

'It's never too late for Christmas!' yelled Dudley, and the other elves cheered.

Santa sat back. He was holding the reins to the sleigh, but the reindeer did not need any direction. They were going home. He felt happier than he had in many years, and as they flew through the sky, the cold ocean many miles below, Santa began to sing:

'It's a frosty night,
All snowy and cold
I'm delivering presents
Before I get old.
I'm wearing my outfit,
I'm driving my sleigh,
It's going to be a wondrous, perfect
Magical Christmas Day!
I ain't got the blues,
No I ain't got the blues,
I'm saying goodbye,
To the Christmas Eve blues.'

The next morning all the children of the world, even the ones who'd been naughty, received a host of presents, magically delivered by Santa Claus in a magically short period of time, early on Christmas morning. And instead of the presents they'd been used to receiving in recent years, the children were all given the types of toys and games that their parents and grandparents had been given. Wooden trains and blocks, hand-crafted board games and dolls' houses, whistles and sticks, puppets and castles. And every gift was filled with the magic of Christmas, and every child who opened a present smelled cinnamon and spices, turkey and pine needles, they heard the ring of silver bells and the laughter of all the other children, and they all, every single one of them, felt warmer than a cup of hot chocolate.

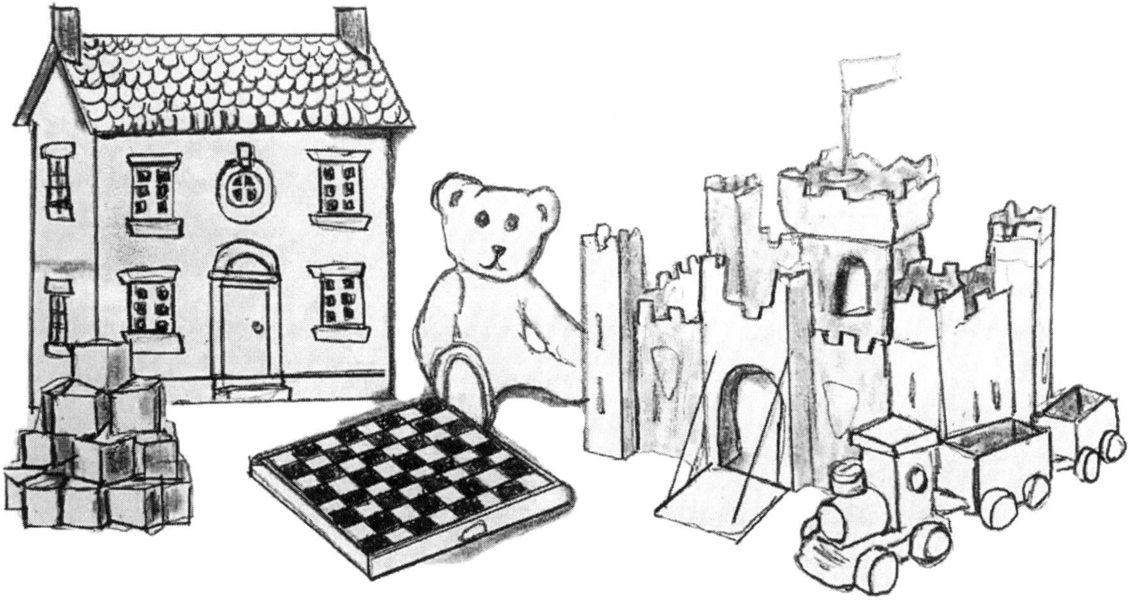

50

Douglas Lindsay lives in Somerset. He is the writer of over fifty books, though sadly none of the others are anything like the one you've just read.

Printed in Great Britain
by Amazon